CONTENTS

CHAPTER 1   THE BLOB *RETOLD* 4

CHAPTER 2   *THE MAKING OF* THE BLOB 16

CHAPTER 3   *BEHIND* THE BLOB 24

CHAPTER 4   THE BLOB *PHENOMENON* 32

FILMOGRAPHY 39

GLOSSARY 42

FOR MORE INFORMATION 44

FOR FURTHER READING AND VIEWING 45

BIBLIOGRAPHY 46

INDEX 47

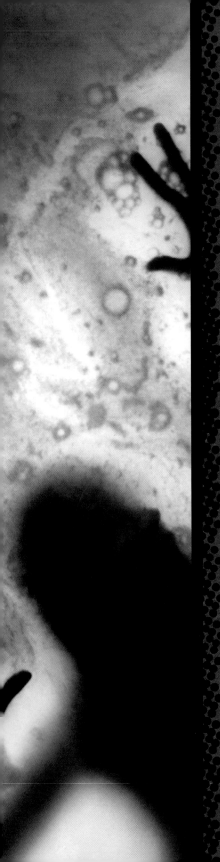

CHAPTER 1

THE BLOB *RETOLD*

Steve Andrews and Jane Martin are two typical eighteen-year-olds out on a date. It's a warm Friday night, and they're sitting in Steve's convertible with the top down. As they talk and kiss, they see a shooting star sail across the evening sky. When they hear a loud boom, they realize that the shooting star must have been a meteorite. And it sounds like it landed nearby! Steve wants to investigate, so he starts up the car, and he and Jane head out to find the meteorite.

Meanwhile, an old man living in a shack in the mountains has heard the noise, too, and he steps out to have a look. The meteorite has landed in his yard, creating a large crater. As the old man peers down into the hole, he spots a smoldering piece of the meteorite. He gets a stick and starts prodding the rock. As it breaks apart, a colorless gooey substance oozes out of the middle. Curious, the old man continues to poke at it, and the goo clings to the stick.

The old man then tilts the stick up so he can get a closer look. When the goo creeps closer to his hand, the man nervously tips the

stick away from him. Even with the stick tilted downward, though, the goo defies gravity and keeps creeping upward. In an instant, it has engulfed the old man's hand! He screams and tries to push the gooey mass off, but it's no use. His entire hand is covered. Furthermore, the goo has now changed from being colorless to a blood-red color, the color of the Blob. Frightened, the old man runs down the hill and into the street, still trying desperately to get the sinister mass off his hand.

Just then, the teens—Steve and Jane—are driving down the road, looking for the place where the meteorite crashed into the earth. What they find instead is the old man stumbling around in the middle of the street, with the Blob feeding off the flesh of his hand. The old man is howling in pain, and he begs the teens to take him to a doctor. Steve and Jane oblige, and the threesome heads off to Dr. Hallen's office in town.

As they approach the office, the doctor is just locking up for the night. But when Steve and Jane explain that it's an emergency, Dr. Hallen agrees to take a look at the old man's hand. Immediately, the doctor sees that the old man's situation is grim. By now, the Blob is covering not only the old man's hand but also his entire arm. The doctor may even need to amputate the arm to save the man's life. Before he does anything, though, Dr. Hallen asks Steve and Jane for their help. He wants them to go back to the place where they met the old man to see if they can find anyone who knows what happened to him. The teens agree to help.

As Steve and Jane head back to the woods, Dr. Hallen telephones his nurse and asks her to return to the office.

Steve (Steve McQueen), Jane (Aneta Corsaut) and Dr. Hallen (Steven Chase) observe the Blob's first victim (Olin Howlin). Most of *The Blob*'s cast were unknown actors with little film experience. Howlin was an exception. He was a character actor who had made nearly 200 movies. *The Blob* would be his last film, as he died about a year after the movie was released.

When she arrives, the doctor asks her to go into the exam room and prepare the old man for surgery. The nurse enters the room, but the patient is gone. Suddenly, the nurse lets out a blood-curdling scream. The mass of goo that was on the old man's arm has now completely consumed him! The Blob has grown much larger, and it's oozing its way over to the nurse.

At the sound of the nurse's scream, Dr. Hallen runs into the exam room. He, too, sees the Blob, which is gigantic. The doctor tells the nurse to throw acid at the Blob. She does as Dr. Hallen orders, but the Blob cannot be stopped! Dr. Hallen rushes into another room to grab his shotgun. By the time he returns, it's too late. The Blob has already consumed the nurse and has quickly grown even more menacing. The doctor shoots the Blob, but bullets don't harm the monster.

In the meantime, on their way back to the woods, Steve and Jane have run into a few friends. When they tell their friends the story about the old man, all the teens decide to help search for clues about what happened to him. As the teens walk through the woods, they come upon an empty shack. Nearby, they find the old man's lantern next to the crater where the meteorite hit. That's when they figure out that the goo that attached itself to the old man's arm must have come from outer space!

As Steve and Jane head back to Dr. Hallen's office to share their discovery, their friends head off to the midnight fright flick that is playing at the local movie theater. When Steve and Jane return to the doctor's office, something seems odd. The office is dark. Steve walks around the out-side of the office and looks in the window. What he sees is a gruesome sight. Dr. Hallen is struggling to get away from the Blob, which is now enormous. But Dr. Hallen is no match for the awful Blob. As Steve watches helplessly from outside, the monster consumes another victim.

Steve is horrified by what he's just witnessed. He returns to the car and tells Jane what has happened and that they

Steve, Jane, and their friends investigate the crater where the meteorite hit. They realize that the Blob came from outer space, but nobody will believe them. Teens who know the truth but are ignored by the adults around them are often the heroes of horror films, including those portrayed in *The Blob*. Young moviegoers of the 1950s flocked to such movies, and teen horror films became a lucrative genre for studios.

have to report it to the police. At the police station, however, no one believes the teens' wild story about the gigantic man-eating Blob from outer space.

The police officers think that the teens' story is just a hoax, but they agree to check Dr. Hallen's office just in case. By the time the officers get to the doctor's office, though, it's a mess, and the Blob has vanished. The police officers believe that the teens have pulled a prank or that they have vandalized the doctor's office. They call Steve and Jane's parents to tell them to pick the teens up and to take them home.

Knowing that the Blob is real—and that it's already killed several people—neither Steve nor Jane can stay put at home. They feel that it's their responsibility to warn the townspeople of the danger. Even though it's the middle of the night, Steve and Jane sneak out of their houses and head back to town. Their first stop is the movie theater, where their friends are still watching the midnight spook show. Steve tells the other teens about the horrible monster

THE BLOB THEME SONG

The theme song for the movie *The Blob* is called "The Blob." The singing credit for "The Blob" is given to the Five Blobs. In reality, though, only one person— Bernie Nee, a studio singer—sang the song. His voice was overdubbed to sound like a group of singers. Composer Burt Bacharach wrote the music. This song-writer went on to write many classic and award-winning songs, including "What the World Needs Now Is Love" (1965) and "Raindrops Keep Fallin' on My Head" (1969). "The Blob" was one of Bacharach's early hits.

Some critics believe that *The Blob* theme song is the perfect introduction to a fun and campy 1950s B movie. Others, however, find its catchy and light-hearted tune as well as its silly lyrics to be a fairly unusual choice for a horror film. Regardless of critics' opinions, the song reached number 33 on the top-40 Billboard music charts for a short time after the film's release in 1958.

that is loose in the town. He instructs them to knock on doors and tell everyone what has happened.

The teens start walking around town, telling people about the Blob. But not one adult will believe their story. As Steve and Jane pass by the grocery store that is owned by Steve's father, they notice that the store looks peculiar. The door is unlocked, although it's long past closing time. Steve and Jane walk inside, calling out to the janitor. Just then, the Blob appears, oozing across the floor toward them and blocking the exits. Jane screams and knocks over a display of canned goods in her haste to get away from the slimy monster.

Steve realizes that their only chance to get away from the Blob is to hide in the meat locker at the back of the store. The teens shut the heavy door behind them, but they still aren't safe. The sinister mass of goo begins to ooze through the small crack under the door! Steve and Jane hold on to each other, sure that this will be their end. However, just as quickly as it appeared under the meat locker door, the Blob retreats, going back from where it had come.

With great relief, Steve and Jane carefully open the door of the meat locker and peek out. The Blob has left the store, and the teens are safe for the moment. Steve and Jane quickly gather their friends together again, and Steve shares his plan. He tells them that they must get the attention of the townspeople. He instructs the teens to make as much noise as possible to wake up the town. Suddenly, the quiet night is filled with the sounds of car horns, fire alarms, and air raid sirens. All the noisemaking works! Throughout the

Steve and Jane hide from the Blob in a meat locker. Steve McQueen had originally been signed to a three-picture deal by *The Blob*'s producers, with *The Blob* being the first of the films. However, the actor proved very difficult to work with, and was released from his contract before making the next two movies.

town, people get out of bed and head outside to see what all the commotion is about.

At the same time, and unknown by the teens, the Blob is attacking its latest victim. It oozes into the projection booth of the movie theater and consumes the projectionist. With no one there to change the film reel, the movie abruptly ends. Just as the audience starts to grow restless, the Blob begins to ominously ooze through the vents from the projection booth down into the theater. As the people in the audience become aware of the monster, they scream and run out of the theater.

Just then, the massive monster oozes onto the street and heads toward the crowd that has gathered there. The Blob has grown larger with each victim, and by this time, it has become enormous. The adults can finally see that the teens were telling the truth the whole time. The monster is real, and it's threatening to consume the entire town!

People start to run in all directions to escape the Blob. Just then, Jane sees her little brother, Danny, among the crowd. Danny runs into the town diner, and Jane and Steve follow him inside. But the Blob has become so huge that it completely covers the diner. Suddenly, the pay phone in the diner rings. On the other end of the line, Lieutenant Dave Barton, the police chief, instructs Steve to get Jane, Danny, and the others to go down into the cellar of the diner. Barton has a plan to destroy the monster.

Outside the diner, the police chief directs a fellow officer to shoot at a power line. The police chief hopes that by dropping a live wire on the Blob, the monster will burn up. The power line sparks and sizzles as it hits the monster, but the Blob is unharmed. Meanwhile, the sparks set the diner on fire, with Steve, Jane, and the others trapped in the

Steve, Jane, Danny, and others seek safety in the diner while the Blob surrounds them on all sides. Though the movie is called *The Blob*, no one ever calls the menacing goo that name in the film. The shooting script referred to it as "the mass," and one of the movie's original titles was *The Glob*.

The townspeople spray the Blob with cold carbon dioxide gas until the monster is completely still. Though the town is saved from the Blob at the end of the movie, the fact that the Blob is not dead, but merely subdued, leaves the door open for the human-eating menace to return in future films.

cellar—and the Blob oozing inside. If the fire doesn't kill them, the Blob surely will!

In a desperate attempt to keep the fire from getting closer, Steve sprays a fire extinguisher. The carbon dioxide gas from the fire extinguisher has a surprising effect. When the ice-cold gas hits the Blob, the menacing monster retreats. That's when Steve makes an amazing discovery—

the Blob doesn't like the cold! Earlier, the monster shrank back from the cold in the meat locker at the grocery store. Now it reacted the same way when it was hit with the cold carbon dioxide gas.

With the phone line still open upstairs in the diner, Steve calls out to Lieutenant Barton who is on the other end of the line. He tells the police chief about the effect that cold carbon dioxide has on the Blob. Barton immediately sends Steve and Jane's friends to the high school, where there are plenty of carbon dioxide fire extinguishers. The teens return quickly, and everyone grabs a fire extinguisher. They spray the Blob with the cold carbon dioxide, and the monster begins to retreat from the diner. Soon, the once-menacing mass of goo is completely still.

Steve, Jane, and the others rush out of the diner to the great relief of their friends and family. Steve is a hero for saving the town from the evil Blob, and no one will doubt his word ever again. But the monster is only frozen, not dead. What will happen when it thaws? After making a phone call, Lieutenant Barton tells Steve and the others that the air force will send a large transport plane to pick up the Blob. The monster will be flown to the icy Arctic, where it will stay frozen forever—or at least for as long as the Arctic remains cold!

CHAPTER 2

THE MAKING OF THE BLOB

The Blob, originally released in 1958, is not your typical Hollywood movie. In fact, not much about *The Blob* is even remotely related to a Hollywood production. It was filmed thousands of miles away from Hollywood, California, in a couple of small towns on the East Coast. Neither the director nor the producer had ever worked on a full-length feature film before. Most of the cast members were not well known and had worked mainly in regional theater. The original budget for the film was $100,000—a miniscule amount even by 1958 standards. *The Blob* was filmed in color, which was very unusual for a low-budget horror film in the 1950s.

LOCATION FILMING

One of the factors that helped keep *The Blob*'s budget low was the location shooting. All the exterior shots for *The Blob* were done on location near the film's production studio. The scenes were filmed primarily in the small towns of Phoenixville and Downingtown in

Pennsylvania. These two neighboring towns are located about twenty miles (thirty-two kilometers) west of Philadelphia.

Many people believe that a large part of *The Blob*'s charm comes from its being filmed in these actual American towns. Unlike many other movies, *The Blob* was not filmed on a Hollywood back lot made to look like a real town. Many of the key buildings from the film, including the doctor's office, the diner, and the movie theater, still exist today. Jerry's Market in Phoenixville—which was used in the movie as the grocery store where Steve and Jane hide from the Blob—is thought to have been destroyed in a fire many years ago.

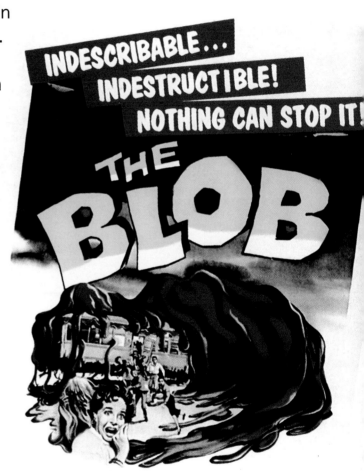

This poster marks the only time Steve McQueen was billed as Steven. Aneta Corsaut's last name is also misspelled. Another mistake occurred in some promotional materials, in which her character is called Judy instead of Jane.

Director Irving S. Yeaworth Jr. poses outside the Colonial Theatre that featured so prominently in *The Blob*, in this 1995 photograph. Though he produced and directed other films throughout the 1950s and 1960s, he is best remembered for his work on *The Blob*. Yeaworth kept a mason jar with a gooey red substance labeled "Blob" in his study.

PRODUCTION CREDITS

By most accounts, Jack H. Harris provided the initial motivation for making *The Blob*. Harris, who is credited as the movie's producer, was a film distributor in the Philadelphia area. He became inspired to make a science-fiction film after seeing *The Thing*, a 1951 sci-fi thriller, now a classic. As a film distributor, Harris saw the growing popularity of both science-fiction and teen delinquency films in the 1950s. He knew that teens represented a large portion of the moviegoing audience, so he decided to make a film that combined these two popular genres.

Harris turned to an associate, Irvin S. Yeaworth Jr., who owned a film production company in Chester Springs, Pennsylvania. Yeaworth was an ordained Methodist minister. His company, Good News Productions, produced short religious educational films. Yeaworth agreed to direct *The Blob*, and he created a new production company called Valley Forge Films to produce secular (nonreligious) films. *The Blob* would be the first feature film for both director Yeaworth and producer Harris.

Although *The Blob*'s original budget was only $100,000, Harris had to raise all the money himself. He took out a second

THE MOLTEN MONSTER

The movie *The Blob* was not always called *The Blob*. When screenwriter Kate Phillips began to work on the script, the original movie title was *The Molten Monster*. At various times, the film was known by other working titles, including *The Molten Meteorite*, *The Meteorite Monster*, and *The Glob*. The film probably would have been titled *The Glob* had there not already been a book with the same title. So the producers decided on *The Blob*, which was similar yet different. Interestingly, none of the characters in the original film or in the sequel or remake that followed the 1958 picture ever referred to the monster as "the blob."

mortgage on his house and borrowed against his own life insurance policy as well as his children's policies. According to Harris, the entire film was shot in about thirty days. The production, including all the film's special effects, took another six months to complete. By the time it was finished, *The Blob* had gone $30,000 over budget, making the final production cost $130,000.

FILM SCRIPT

The original idea for *The Blob* came from Irvine H. Millgate, Jack H. Harris's friend. At first, the script was nothing more than a few pages of scribbled notes. Ted Simonson, an employee of Valley Forge Films, fleshed out the story. Then the production company brought in Kate Phillips. She was a former film actress who had become a professional screen-writer for television. Although she had never seen a science-fiction film, Phillips took the pieces of the story and wove them together into a polished script. She spent two weeks working on the screenplay and received $125 for her efforts. Phillips and Simonson received credit as cowriters of *The Blob*.

THE ACTORS

Most of the actors in *The Blob* had appeared mainly in plays in the New York City and Philadelphia areas. One exception was Olin Howlin, who played the role of the old man who became the Blob's first victim. Howlin was a character actor who had appeared in nearly 200 movies, some dating back to the silent film era of the early 1900s. The character of the old man in *The Blob* became Olin Howlin's final film role. He died about a year after the movie was released.

The two main characters in *The Blob*—teens Steve Andrews and Jane Martin—were played by Steve McQueen and Aneta Corsaut. *The Blob* was the only film in which Steve McQueen was billed as Steven McQueen. It was the first and only time that he played a character named Steve, and it was his first and last monster movie.

STEVE MCQUEEN

Although Steve McQueen was playing an eighteen-year-old in the movie, he was actually twenty-seven at the time. He had appeared in two earlier films, but *The Blob* was his first leading role. For his work on *The Blob*, McQueen was reportedly paid the sum of $3,000. (In comparison, some top movie stars today earn $25 million per

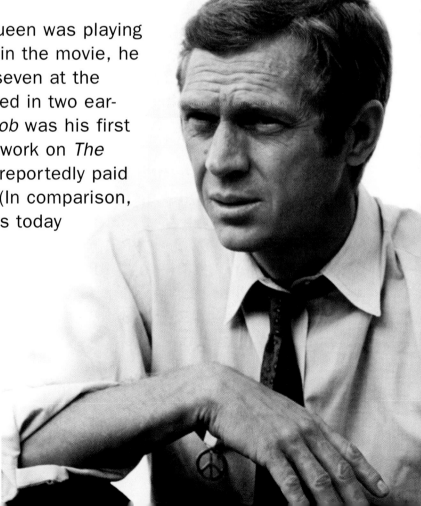

Steve McQueen was the only cast member of *The Blob* to achieve cinematic stardom. After his role in the smash horror film, he went on to star in such classics as *The Magnificent Seven*, *The Great Escape*, and *Bullitt* before his death in 1980.

film!) The story goes that McQueen opted for the cash instead of a share in the film's profits. Surely he regretted that decision after *The Blob* went on to earn millions of dollars at the box office.

Of all the actors who appeared in *The Blob*, Steve McQueen was the only one to achieve major movie stardom. After completing *The Blob*, he starred in a television show, a Western, called *Wanted: Dead or Alive*, which ran from 1958 to 1961. Both the film and the TV show helped launch McQueen's career. He went on to star in many popular and well-respected films, including *The Magnificent Seven* (1960), *The Great Escape* (1963), and *Bullitt* (1968). McQueen became famous for his on- and off-screen persona as a loner, an outsider, a rebel, and a reluctant hero. His role as Steve Andrews in *The Blob* marked the beginning of that perception.

ANETA CORSAUT

As Steve McQueen had been, actress Aneta Corsaut was much older than the eighteen-year-old character she played in *The Blob*. According to one account, McQueen and Corsaut had actually dated in real life before playing boyfriend and girlfriend in the movie. *The Blob* was Corsaut's first feature film. Although she did not act in many movies after *The Blob*, she did go on to have a long career in television.

Corsaut's most famous role was as Helen Crump, the schoolteacher and girlfriend of Sheriff Andy Taylor on *The Andy Griffith Show* during the late 1960s. Corsaut also

Aneta Corsaut, pictured here with Andy Griffith in a still from *The Andy Griffith Show*, had a long and successful career in television. Aside from her role as Helen Crump on *The Andy Griffith Show*, she appeared in such shows as *Columbo*, *Days of Our Lives*, and *Matlock*.

guest-starred on many other television shows from the 1950s through the 1980s. She even made a couple of guest appearances on *Matlock* in the late 1980s. That television show featured her former costar, Andy Griffith.

CHAPTER 3

BEHIND THE BLOB

Some movie monsters have literary origins. Dr. Frankenstein's monster first appeared in Mary Wollstonecraft Shelley's novel *Frankenstein, or the Modern Prometheus*, which was published in 1818. The vampire Count Dracula came to life in the pages of Bram Stoker's 1897 novel, entitled *Dracula*. Comic books, myths and legends, and even real-life events have inspired the creation of other movie monsters. However, the Blob does not fit into any of these categories. The Blob also differs from other movie monsters of the 1950s in that it has no human traits. Most other movie monsters from this era, including the Mummy, the Wolf Man, and the Creature from the Black Lagoon, are at least partially human. The Blob doesn't look or act in any way like a human being. Its only motivation seems to be to consume its next victim.

The Blob is an original monster created just for the movies. The origin of this creature is more of a reflection of the time period in which it was created than any specific source. The Blob monster was invented specifically to appeal to—and scare the daylights out of—moviegoers in the 1950s. The events of that time period played an important role in the creation of the Blob—both the monster and the movie.

TELEVISION VS. MOVIES

During the decade of the 1950s, the number of television sets in American homes rose from about 6 million in 1950 to 60 million in 1960. Although television broadcasting in the United States had begun in 1939, it was suspended in 1941 when the country entered into World War II. Television broadcasting resumed after the war ended in 1945. As the medium of television began to reach more people, its popularity began to rise.

During those early years, television's success had a negative effect on the film industry. Many people were content to stay at home watching TV rather than spend money going out to a movie theater to watch films. The majority of people who still went out to the movies were young. In the 1950s, more than 70 percent of moviegoers were between the ages of twelve and twenty-five.

THE TEEN AUDIENCE

Film studios quickly realized that they needed to produce movies that would appeal to teens—the biggest moviegoing audience. During the 1950s, juvenile delinquency films were very popular among teenage moviegoers. These films

Movies about troubled teenagers became very popular in the 1950s. Pictured here are Natalie Wood and James Dean in a scene from *Rebel Without a Cause*, perhaps the most famous of the juvenile delinquency films of the 1950s. Teenagers were becoming more important as a demographic audience, and movie studios responded by producing dramas and horror films that would appeal to young moviegoers.

included *Rebel Without a Cause* and *Blackboard Jungle*, both released in 1955.

With teens as the main characters, *The Blob* was written to appeal to 1950s youths. As teenagers in juvenile delinquency films did, the teens in *The Blob* feel alienated from the adults in the story. The adults don't take the teens seriously until it's almost too late. In the end, though, it's the teens who save the town from the monster.

Not only did the teen audience of the 1950s like seeing movies about people their own age, but they also enjoyed being scared. That is why science-fiction and horror movies were so popular with them. On this level, too, *The Blob* was written with teen moviegoers in mind. Horror films also tended to be inexpensive to produce. The low cost of making horror movies attracted independent movie studios, such as *The Blob*'s Valley Forge Films, to that genre.

DRIVE-IN THEATERS

Another boon to the movie industry of the 1950s was the steady increase in the number of automobiles being produced by car manufacturers. More car owners meant more drive-in theaters, which had sprouted up all over the country. By 1958, drive-ins had reached their peak of popularity with more than 4,000 in the United States. Teenagers made up the majority of people in the audiences of drive-in theaters.

Going to the movies has always been a favorite pastime for teens. Drive-ins became a popular place for teens to take their dates. The large film studios could not produce enough movies to keep up with the demand created by all the new drive-in theaters. This is another reason why there was room for small, independent movie studios to produce films such as *The Blob*. These low-budget horror films may have been schlocky and campy, but teen audiences in the 1950s flocked to see them.

THE BIRTH OF *THE BLOB*

The monster in *The Blob* is a remarkable creation. Credit for giving life to the Blob goes to the special-effects team at Valley Forge Films, the movie's production company. By today's standards, of course, the special effects seem pretty amateurish. But considering that the film was made in the 1950s, and given its small budget, the special effects are actually quite inventive.

To create the Blob, the film's producers consulted a chemical manufacturing company. They needed a substance that would move like the Blob and could be easily manipulated. The chemical company had created silicone in liquid form, and it turned out to be just the right substance with which to create the Blob. Silicone is normally clear, so red coloring was added to turn the Blob blood red after it began consuming human flesh. The special-effects people had only one problem: the color kept separating. They had to mix the silicone several times each day so that the red coloring did not settle to the bottom.

The Blob was made of silicone mixed with red coloring. Though the Blob appears huge at certain points in the film, only two gallons of the substance were actually used in the movie.

The Blob is actually quite small—only about 2 gallons (7.6 liters) of the substance were used to film the movie. To make the Blob appear large on screen, the special-effects team created miniature sets. For a few scenes, including one in the doctor's office, they used a modified weather balloon to create the Blob. The partially inflated weather balloon was covered with the colored silicone. Then it was manipulated from underneath to look as if the monster was moving by itself.

FEAR OF COMMUNISM

Following the end of World War II, the Soviet Union and the United States entered a period known as the Cold War. During the 1950s, there was a great deal of hostility between Communist countries, such as the Soviet Union, and non-Communist countries, such as the United States. Many Americans became concerned about the threat of Communism. They feared that Communism might even spread to the United States.

Some people have suggested that the Blob monster is actually an allegory about Communism. The Blob devours everything in its path and, as a result, grows larger and more destructive with every meal. Some people see similar qualities in the spread of Communism. During the 1950s, Americans worried that the Soviet Union would invade other countries and that Communism would spread throughout the world. They viewed Communism, in which individuals lose many of their personal freedoms, as a serious threat to American democracy. The fear of Communism was sometimes called the Red Scare or the Red Menace because red is the color most often associated with Communism and the Soviet Union. The Blob's red color is often said to suggest Communist or Soviet symbolism.

NEW FRONTIERS

Major events that took place during the 1950s had forever changed the world. These events also influenced the creation

On October 4, 1957, the Soviet Union launched *Sputnik I*, the first human-made satellite to orbit Earth. New innovations in space technology, such as satellites, interested many people, and science fiction became very popular. Thus, the Blob's otherworldly origins appealed to the imaginations of many Americans, who were both intrigued and frightened by the idea of space exploration.

of *The Blob* and other films of the era. For one, new technology had allowed both the Soviet Union, in 1957, and the United States, in 1958, to launch satellites into the space beyond Earth's atmosphere.

People around the world became intrigued with the idea of space exploration. It now seemed entirely possible that human beings might someday meet aliens from outer space.

This exciting yet scary idea spurred the imaginations of many people. Filmmakers wondered about the new world of outer space and about the possibility of an alien invasion. They created the Blob and the other alien monsters that appeared in 1950s horror movies as a way to explore this possibility.

Although technology allowed humans to explore the new frontier of outer space, it also enabled great destruction in the form of the atomic bomb. The new nuclear age prompted extreme concerns about the scientific unknown. Many film monsters invented during the 1950s were a reflection of these concerns.

CHAPTER 4

THE BLOB *PHENOMENON*

Amid a sea of low-budget, low-tech horror movies from the 1950s, *The Blob* stands out from the crowd. Over the years, the film has developed a cult following of fans and has turned into something of a phenomenon. *The Blob* has been reissued many times since its initial release in 1958, including a collector's edition DVD in 2000.

Most people do not consider *The Blob* to be one of the greatest films of all time. For fans of the horror and science-fiction movie genres, however, *The Blob* is often considered a classic. As proof of *The Blob*'s influence, it spawned a sequel in 1972, and a remake thirty years after the original film was released. Some people even believe that *The Blob* inspired the creation of other movie monsters, including the slimy aliens in the 1984 science-fiction comedy *Ghostbusters*. There have also been dozens of jokes, parodies, and imitators of *The Blob*.

BLOB REVIEWS AND REVENUE

Following the release of *The Blob* in 1958, most critics were not especially fond of this independently produced, low-budget teen fright flick. One critic of the day said that *The Blob* was "a crawling roomful of Jell-O that eats you instead of the other way around." Another critic was even less kind, calling the film "not so much horror as horrid." The film critic from the *New York Herald Tribune* was one of the few to give *The Blob* high marks. Paul V. Beckley wrote that the movie has "a monster with propensities that will curdle the dreams." He also called *The Blob* "a minor classic in its field."

Movie audiences disagreed with the negative critics, though, and the film was an instant hit. *The Blob* had been sold to Paramount Pictures. Originally, it was supposed to be released as the second-billed film in a double feature with *I Married a Monster from Outer Space*. Paramount soon realized, though, that the majority of moviegoers were actually going to the double feature to see *The Blob*. The studio quickly switched the billing, making *The Blob* the top-billed film.

In his 2003 book, *Hollywood Horror: From Gothic to Cosmic*, author Mark A. Vieira discussed *The Blob*'s popularity. He explained why the audience did not mind that the acting was not always first rate and that the film lacked Hollywood polish. "[Producer Jack H. Harris] had purposely made teenagers the heroes of the film, and teenagers were his audience," wrote Vieira. He added, "*The Blob* ultimately grossed one hundred times its cost."

BLOB SEQUEL

In 1972, Jack H. Harris, the original producer of *The Blob*, produced a sequel called *Beware! The Blob*. Also known as

BLOBFEST

Located in Phoenixville, Pennsylvania, the Colonial Theatre is a real movie theater that was made famous by *The Blob*. During a pivotal scene in the 1958 film, the theater plays a prominent role. The teens in the film are watching the midnight spook show double feature at this theater. When the sinister Blob starts to ooze through the vents in the theater, the audience runs screaming from the building, trying to get away from the evil monster.

Today, the Colonial Theatre looks very much like it did when *The Blob* was filmed. Each summer, the theater holds an annual BlobFest to celebrate the movie that made it famous. The weekend of festivities includes several showings of *The Blob*, a costume contest, and a street festival featuring food, music, and vintage cars. Attendees at BlobFest can even view a piece of the original Blob that is on display. The highlight of BlobFest, though, is probably a reenactment of the scene from the film in which the audience runs out of the theater to escape the Blob. Each year, several hundred people participate in this event.

This 2002 photograph shows audiences leaving the Colonial Theatre after a screening of *The Blob*. In the film's pivotal scene in which viewers run out of the theater as the Blob nears, many extras can be seen laughing and smiling on camera.

A worker (Godfrey Cambridge) in a scientific facility brings home a sample of the Blob, which his wife (Marlene Clark) accidentally thaws. Thus begins *Beware! The Blob*, a sequel to the original that was directed by Larry Hagman.

Son of Blob, the film was directed by Larry Hagman, who was also an actor. Hagman had starred in the television show *I Dream of Jeannie* in the late 1960s. *Beware! The Blob* was reissued after Hagman achieved fame playing J. R. Ewing on the popular television show *Dallas* during the 1980s. In a famous *Dallas* cliffhanger episode, an unseen attacker fired a gun at Hagman's character. Viewers around the world wanted to know, "Who shot J. R.?" For its reissue, *Beware! The Blob* was cleverly touted as "The Movie That J. R. Shot!" since Hagman had directed it.

In *Beware! The Blob*, starring Robert Walker Jr., a scientist brings home a piece of the original Blob that was frozen in the Arctic. When the monster is accidentally thawed, it begins to terrorize a small town. Much like in the original film, a teen must save the day. *Beware! The Blob* did not achieve a great deal of critical success. Even producer Jack H. Harris admitted that this sequel ended up being more funny than scary.

BLOB REMAKE

In 1988, Chuck Russell directed a remake of *The Blob*. The previous year, Russell had directed *A Nightmare on Elm Street 3: Dream Warriors*. The plot of *The Blob* remake was similar to that of the original film. With a reported budget of between $17 million and $18 million, though, the remake's special effects were much more high-tech and decidedly more graphic. According to *People Weekly*, "Chuck Russell's Blob may be the most sinister slime of all time."

In the original 1958 film, blood and violence were left mostly to the audience's imagination. With director Chuck Russell at the helm, the 1988 *Blob* remake was a spine-tingling horror film with no-holds-barred guts and gore. Janet Maslin, film critic for the *New York Times*, called the remake "a lively, grisly, better-than-average high-tech monster movie that devotes more energy to special effects than to drama."

Actress Candy Clark comes face to face with the all-consuming mass in this 1988 version of *The Blob*. Though the remake shared a similar story to that of the original, the later film's special effects were more advanced. For the film's ending, rock salt was dyed purple to create the crystallized Blob that appears in the final scenes.

THE BLOB'S LASTING APPEAL

For a very low-budget 1950s monster movie, the original *The Blob* has had a surprisingly long-lasting appeal. What accounts for *The Blob*'s staying power? In *Science Fiction Confidential*, author Tom Weaver interviewed Kate Phillips, one of *The Blob*'s screenwriters. She believed that timing and originality were key elements in the film's box-office success. Phillips said, "[*The Blob*] came out just at the right time . . . Until that time, the monsters [in 1950s monster movies] had been mechanical things or giants. There hadn't been anything nearly like *The Blob*."

In *Science Fiction Confidential*, Weaver also interviewed Russ Doughten, one of *The Blob*'s producers. Doughten also believed that originality is a major factor in the film's continuing appeal. He said, "I think there's a freshness to *The Blob* because it was a truly original story and the characters in it were approached as original people."

In his 1972 book, *Monsters from the Movies*, author Thomas G. Aylesworth noted that some fans of monster movies considered *The Blob* to be one of the best of its genre. Aylesworth suggested that it might have been Steve McQueen's fine performance in the lead role that made *The Blob* noteworthy. Aylesworth wrote, "Or perhaps it is the small-town atmosphere of the picture that makes it more scary. We can believe that monsters go to the city more readily than we will accept the creature who attacked a small town."

Regardless of the reasons for its popularity, *The Blob* remains a standout in a huge field of monster movies and movie monsters. Even with today's high-budget, high-tech science-fiction thrillers, *The Blob* has kept its cult following for decades. There is no doubt it will continue to thrill and delight movie audiences for generations to come.

FILMOGRAPHY

THE BLOB

Beware! The Blob (1972) Directed by Larry Hagman, this movie was also known as *Son of Blob.* In the film, a technician brings back a piece of the Blob from the North Pole. When his wife accidentally thaws the slab, the monster begins to devour the town.

Blobermouth (1990) A comedy directed by Kent Skov, this film portrays an animated talking Blob as a stand-up comic pitted against rival comedian Steve McQueen. For this movie, a comedy group's members dubbed their own voices with this new story line over the original 1958 film.

The Blob (1958) The tagline for the original movie says it all: "Indescribable . . . Indestructible! Nothing Can Stop It!"

The Blob (1988) In this remake of the 1958 movie, directed by Chuck Russell, the Blob is a creation of a secret government chemical-warfare program that goes horribly wrong. Teenagers try to warn the townspeople, but no one will believe them. Meanwhile, the government tries to cover up its activities.

STEVE MCQUEEN (1930–1980)

The Hunter (1980)
Tom Horn (1980)

An Enemy of the People (1978)
The Towering Inferno (1974)
Papillon (1973)
The Getaway (1972)
Junior Bonner (1972)
Le Mans (1971)
The Reivers (1969)
Bullitt (1968)
The Thomas Crown Affair (1968)
The Sand Pebbles (1966)
Nevada Smith (1966)
The Cincinnati Kid (1965)
Baby the Rain Must Fall (1965)
Love with the Proper Stranger (1963)
Soldier in the Rain (1963)
The Great Escape (1963)
The War Lover (1962)
Hell Is for Heroes (1962)
The Honeymoon Machine (1961)
The Magnificent Seven (1960)
The Great St. Louis Bank Robbery (1960)
Never So Few (1959)
Wanted: Dead or Alive (1958–1961) TV series
The Blob (1958)
Never Love a Stranger (1958)
Somebody Up There Likes Me (1956)

ANETA CORSAUT (1933–1995)

Matlock: The Suspect (1991) TV movie

Return to Mayberry (1986) TV movie
Days of Our Lives (1984) TV series
House Calls (1979) TV series
The Toolbox Murders (1978)
Bad Ronald (1974) TV movie
Columbo: A Stitch in Crime (1973) TV movie
The Andy Griffith Show (1964–1968) TV series
Good Neighbor Sam (1964)
The Gertrude Berg Show (1961) TV series
The Blob (1958)

GLOSSARY

alienate To separate an individual from something to which the person was previously attached.

allegory An instance in which an artwork or a story's content stands for abstract ideas that suggest a parallel, deeper, or symbolic meaning.

amputate To remove by cutting.

atomic Of or relating to atoms; nuclear.

Cold War An intense ideological struggle and rivalry between the United States and the Soviet Union following World War II.

Communism An economic and governmental system based on common ownership of the means of production and an equal distribution of wealth. In Communism, property is owned by the state in common for all the people.

delinquency Actions that are not considered acceptable behavior or that are against the law.

democracy A system of government in which representatives of the people are elected by the people.

drive-in theater An outdoor establishment where people can watch a movie while sitting in their car.

genre A category of theatrical composition characterized by a particular style.

meteorite A small piece of matter in the solar system that falls to Earth.

phenomenon An exceptional or unusual occurrence.

sequel The next installment of a book or film.

silicone A chemical substance known for its flexibility as well as its water and heat resistance.

technology The application of scientific knowledge, methods, or processes to achieve industrial or commercial goals.

FOR MORE INFORMATION

American Film Institute
2021 N. Western Avenue
Los Angeles, CA 90027-1657
(323) 856-7600
Web Site: http://www.afi.com/

WEB SITES

Due to the changing nature of Internet links, the Rosen
Publishing Group, Inc., has developed an online list of Web
sites related to the subject of this book. This site is updated
regularly. Please use this link to access the list:

http://www.rosenlinks.com/famm/mebl

FOR FURTHER READING AND VIEWING

The Blob. DVD. Criterion Collection, 2000.

Buller, Laura. *Myths and Monsters: From Dragons to Werewolves*. New York: DK Publishing, Inc., 2003.

Frankenstein, Monsters, and Mad Scientists. VHS. Plymouth, MN: Simitar Entertainment, 1996.

Haycock, Kate. *Science Fiction Films*. New York: Crestwood House, 1991.

Hollywood Aliens and Monsters. VHS. New York: A&E Home Video, 1996.

The Horror of It All. VHS. New York: Brighton Video, 1987.

Nottridge, Rhoda. *Horror Films*. New York: Crestwood House, 1991.

Powers, Tom. *Horror Movies*. Minneapolis: Lerner Publications Company, 1989.

Powers, Tom. *Movie Monsters*. Minneapolis: Lerner Publications Company, 1989.

Staskowski, Andrea. *Science Fiction Movies*. Minneapolis: Lerner Publications Company, 1992.

Thorne, Ian. *The Blob*. Mankato, MN: Crestwood House, Inc., 1982.

BIBLIOGRAPHY

Aylesworth, Thomas G. *Monsters from the Movies*. Philadelphia: J. B. Lippincott Company, 1972.

Blob, The. DVD. Criterion Collection, 2000.

"Chuck Russell's Blob May Be the Most Sinister Slime of All Time." *People Weekly*, August 29, 1988, page 114.

Internet Movie Database. "The Blob." Retrieved April 7, 2004 (http://www.imdb.com/title/tt0051418).

Maslin, Janet. "The Blob, Modernized." *New York Times*, August 5, 1988.

St. Charnez, Casey. *The Complete Films of Steve McQueen*. New York: Citadel Press, 1992.

Vieira, Mark A. *Hollywood Horror: From Gothic to Cosmic*. New York: Harry N. Abrams, Inc., 2003.

Weaver, Tom. *Science Fiction Confidential*. Jefferson, NC: McFarland & Co., Inc., 2002.

Wright, Dennis J. "Running of the Blob." *The Phoenixville News*, July 12, 2003.

INDEX

A
allegory, 29
aliens, 30
Andy Griffith Show, The, 22
atomic bomb, 31
Aylesworth, Thomas G., 38

B
Beckley, Paul V., 33
Beware! The Blob, 33, 35
Blackboard Jungle, 26
budget, 16, 20
Bullitt, 22

C
cast members, 16
  Corsaut, Aneta, 21–22
  Howlin, Olin, 20–21
  McQueen, Steve, 21–22
Cold War, 29
color film, 16
comic books, 24
Communism, 29
Creature from the Black Lagoon, the, 24
critics, 33
Crump, Helen, 22

D
Dallas, 35
director, 16
Doughten, Russ, 38
Downingtown, Pennsylvania, 16
Dracula, 24
drive-in theaters, 27

E
exterior shots, 16

Ewing, J. R., 35

F
film industry, 25–27
*Frankenstein, or the Modern
  Prometheus*, 24

G
Ghostbusters, 32
Good News Productions, 19
Great Escape, The, 22
Griffith, Andy, 23

H
Hagman, Larry, 35–36
Harris, Jack H., 18–20, 33, 36
*Hollywood Horror: From Gothic to
  Cosmic*, 33

I
I Dream of Jeannie, 35
*I Married a Monster from Outer
  Space*, 33
independent movie studios, 26–27

J
Jerry's Market, 17
juvenile delinquency films, 25–26

L
location shooting, 16

M
Magnificent Seven, The, 22
Maslin, Janet, 36
Matlock, 23
Millgate, Irvine H., 20

Monsters from the Movies, 38
Mummy, the, 24

N
*Nightmare on Elm Street 3: Dream
    Warriors, A*, 36

P
Paramount Pictures, 33
Phillips, Kate, 20, 37–38
Phoenixville, Pennsylvania, 16–17
producers, 16, 18, 33, 38
production schedule, 20
production studio, 16

R
Rebel Without a Cause, 26
remake, 32, 36
        budget of, 36
Russell, Chuck, 36

S
satellites, 30
Science Fiction Confidential, 37–38
script, 20

sequel, 33, 35
Simonson, Ted, 20
Son of Blob, 35
space exploration, 30
synopsis, 4–15

T
Taylor, Sheriff Andy, 22
teens, 25–27, 36
television, 25
Thing, The, 18

V
Valley Forge Films, 19–20, 27
Vieira, Mark A., 33

W
Walker, Robert, Jr., 36
Wanted: Dead or Alive, 22
Weaver, Tom, 37–38
Wolf Man, the, 24
World War II, 25, 29

Y
Yeaworth, Irvin S., Jr., 19

ABOUT THE AUTHOR

Suzanne J. Murdico is a freelance writer who has written more than twenty books for children and teens. She lives near Tampa, Florida, with her husband, Vinnie, and their cats, Max and Boo.

PHOTO CREDITS

Cover, pp. 1, 4, 6, 8, 11, 13, 14, 16, 17, 23, 24, 26, 32, 35, 37 © The Everett Collection; pp. 18, 28, 34 © AP/Wide World Photos; p. 21 © CinemaPhoto/Corbis; p. 30 © Bettmann/Corbis.

Designer and Illustrations: Tom Forget; Editor: Kathy Kuhtz Campbell